The YALDAH YEAR

Crafts & Recipes for Every Month of the Jewish Year

by Leah Larson & Chavie Resnick

YM Books
P.O. Box 215
Sharon, MA 02067
info@ymbooks.org
www.ymbooks.org

ISBN: 978-0-9841624-1-3

Copyright © 2009 by YM Books*

All rights reserved. No part of this book may be reproduced or transmitted in any form or by any means (electronic, photocopying, recording or otherwise) without prior written permission of the copyright holder.

Cover, book design and photographs by Leah Larson

Manufactured in the United States of America

*YM Books is an imprint of YALDAH Media, Inc.

TABLE OF CONTENTS

Tishrei 5
Sukkah Dazzler 6
Moist Honey Cake 8
Sweet Potato Pie 9

Cheshvan 10
Mezuzah Cover 11
Chicken Soup 12
Chocolate Chip Cookies 14

Kislev 15
Mirrored Menorah 16
Latke Shapes 18
Chocolate Snowballs 19

Tevet 20
Classic Rugelach 22
Apple Kugel 22
Shabbat Candlestick 24

Shevat 25
Broccoli Trees 26
Date Nut Bread 28
Striped Pot 29

Adar 29
Themed Mishloach Manot 31
Hamentashen 32
Gefilte "Fishies" 34

Nissan 35
Fantastic Fruit Salad 36
Easy Meringues 37
Seder Plate 38

Iyar 40
Omer Counter 41
S'more Cupcakes 42
Veggie Kabobs 44

Sivan 45
Blintz Loaf 46
Cheesecake Bars 47
Mosaic Placemat 48

Tammuz 50
Memory Frame 51
Jam Diagonals 52
Chicken Salad 54

Av 55
Sunshine Salad 56
Strawberry Splash 57
Rainbow Tote 58

Elul 60
Pasta Salad 61
Fabric Pushka 62
Marble Cake 64

Welcome to **The YALDAH Year!** In this book we've put together some of our favorite crafts and recipes and given you a few to try each month. Some of them are specifically connected to a holiday in that month, and others are great for all year round. Everything in this book is 'girl friendly' - it's written, tested, photographed, and even designed by Jewish girls like you.

The Jewish months are extra-connected to Jewish girls and women. The Jewish calendar follows the moon, and each month begins with the 'New Moon', when you can hardly see the moon. The New Moon is actually a special holiday called "Rosh Chodesh" or "The Head of the Month". Rosh Chodesh was the first Mitzvah given to the Jewish people, and it's a holiday especially for Jewish women. So at the beginning of each month, take time to celebrate! Celebrate being a Jewish girl, and connect with the special meaning in the upcoming month.

In addition to the fun crafts and recipes, we've also shared some of our thoughts about each Jewish month, as well as great dates of important events that happened in each month throughout Jewish history.

So get ready for your journey through "**The YALDAH Year**"!

Tishrei תשרי

Sometimes the High Holidays feel like a marathon. We're running from Rosh Hashanah to Yom Kippur to Sukkot...dancing to Simchat Torah. It seems like a few weeks straight of family meals, synagogue, and celebrating. Couldn't Hashem have spread the holidays a little more evenly throughout the year?

That's just the point. We're starting off the year with a bang. Standing at the starting line all these holidays get us excited and inspired for the upcoming year. On Rosh Hashanah we celebrate with family and resolve to spend more time with family. That feeling of awe and holiness on Yom Kippur inspires us to be better this year. The joy of Sukkot and Simchat Torah bring joy into the whole year.

It's up to us to let all these holidays affect the rest of the year. We can just float through them and not really absorb any of it. Or, we can take all those powerful feelings we experience during the High Holidays and translate them into practical resolutions.

How are you going to take the holiday spirit with you throughout the year?

What resolutions are you making to make this year the best year yet?

Great Dates!

1 - *Rosh Hashanah*
   Adam & Chava created
   Noach sent last dove from ark
   Akeidat Yitzchak, Sara Imeinu's passing
3 - *Gedalya assassinated - fast day*
5 - *Rabbi Akiva captured by Romans*
8 - *First Beit Hamikdash dedicated*
10 - *Yom Kippur*
   Rivkah Imeinu born
15 - *Sukkot*
22 - *Shemini Atzeret*
23 - *Simchat Torah*

Beaded Sukkah Dazzler

Materials:
Clear fishing line
Different Sized Beads
Ribbon
Scissors

Directions:
1. Cut the fishing line to the length you want the dazzler to be.
2. Tie a bead on the end of each strand of fishing line, so the beads don't fall off. String the bead onto the line, alternating between groups of smaller and larger beads.
3. When you've finished a strand, tie a strong knot around a bead at the end.
4. Cut a ribbon to the width of your Sukkah entrance, or the place where you'd like to hang the dazzler. Lay the ribbon horizontally and tie the fishing line so it hangs off of it vertically. Now you can nail both ends of the ribbon into your Sukkah doorway and have a beautiful beaded decoration!

This craft adds sparkle to any Sukkah -- especially when the sun shines on it!

7

Honey cake is a classic Rosh Hashanah food to start the year off with a sweet start.

Moist Honey Cake

Pareve/Dairy

Ingredients:
3 eggs
1 1/4 cups honey
1 1/2 cups sugar
1 cup liquid coffee
2 teaspoons baking powder
3 tablespoons butter or margarine, softened
4 cups flour
1 teaspoon baking soda
2 teaspoons cinnamon

Directions:
1. Preheat the oven to 325°.
2. Grease a 9x13-inch cake pan, and set aside.
3. In a large bowl, beat the eggs and honey together with a fork or whisk. Pour in the sugar and mix it.
4. In a medium-sized bowl, mix the coffee with the baking powder. Add the margarine. Add to the honey mixture.
5. In a separate bowl mix the flour, baking soda, and cinnamon together. Carefully add this mixture, little by little, to the honey mixture. Blend until smooth.
6. Pour into greased pan and bake for 55 minutes to an hour, or until toothpick comes out clean.

Yields: 1 cake

Sweet-Potato Pie

Pareve/Dairy

Ingredients:
- 3 medium-sized sweet potatoes, baked
- 1 cup soy milk (or milk to make recipe dairy)
- 3 eggs
- 1/2 cup sugar
- 1/4 cup flour
- 2 teaspoons cinnamon
- 1 ready-to-bake pie-crust

Directions:
1. Preheat oven to 400°.
2. In a large bowl, mash sweet potatoes well. Add soy milk or milk, sugar, flour, eggs, and cinnamon.
3. Mix until smooth (you can use an electric mixer for an extra-smooth texture). Pour batter into crust.
4. Bake for 10 minutes, then lower temperature to 350° and bake for 40 more minutes.

Yields: 10 to 12 servings

Cheshvan חשון

Do you know why in Israel they wait until the 7th of Cheshvan to pray for rain, when it's 15 days after the end of Sukkot? In the times of the Beit Hamikdash, all the Jews would come to Yerushalayim for Sukkot. For Jews who lived closer to Yerushalayim, it only took a few days to travel back to their homes. But the Jews who lived the farthest didn't get home until the 7th of Cheshvan. The Jewish people didn't pray for rain, even though they depended on it for crops, until they knew every single Jew was back home and wouldn't have a hard time traveling because of rain. Imagine that! The whole nation gives up the rain they need for their farms, so that a few Jews don't get wet.

A few days later, the 11th of Cheshvan, is Rachel Imeinu's Yartzeit. Rachel also gave up something for the sake of another. When Rachel agreed to marry Yaakov Avinu, they both knew that her father Lavan might try to trick him into marrying Rachel's older sister Leah instead. So they made up signs to give to each other at the wedding. When the day of the wedding came, and Rachel saw Lavan preparing Leah for the wedding, Rachel realized how embarrassed Leah would be if she didn't know the secret signs. Rachel told Leah the signs, saving her from embarrassment, but giving up her chance to marry Yaakov.

That's how much we have to care about others. Sometimes we even have to give up what we want in order to help someone else.

What will you do to show someone how much you care for them?

Great Dates!

7 - Last Jew would come home from Beit Hamikdash
11 - Rachel Imeinu's Yartzeit
15 - Yartzeit of Matityahu - father of Maccabees
17 - Flood began

Mezuzah Cover

Materials:
Sculpey clay in all the colors you plan on using
Toothpicks
Tinfoil
An oven

It's traditional to put the letter "Shin" on Mezuzah covers

Directions:
1. Choose a clay color for the background of your mezuzah cover. Roll it flat (either with a rolling pin or your fingers). Make sure it's bigger than a normal sized mezuzah cover (we'll trim it afterwards).
2. With your other colors, add details. For our tree we added brown branches and leaves. Keep most of your design in the center because that will be the front.
3. Using a toothpick, carve designs or lines into your piece.
4. Add a Hebrew letter 'shin' (see above).
5. Roll a piece of tinfoil until it's the size of the mezuzah scroll you plan on putting inside (around 4 inches tall by 1 inch wide). This will keep your mezuzah cover the right size.
6. Place the tinfoil 'scroll' in the middle, and fold up all four sides of clay to create a box. If some of the sides crack, gently mold them back together.
7. Pinch all the sides and corners so they are strongly stuck together.
8. Using a table knife (with an adult's help) trim all the sides so the mezuzah cover will lay flat.
9. Make 2 small, flat circles of clay. Attach these to the top and bottom of the mezuzah. Using a toothpick, make a hole big enough for a nail on each end.
10. Flip your mezuzah cover back over and make sure it lies flat. Keep the tinfoil 'scroll' inside. Cover a cookie-sheet with tinfoil. Lay the mezuzah cover on top.
11. With an adult's help, bake at 275° for 15-20 minutes.
12. Let the mezuzah cover cool completely. Gently remove the tinfoil scroll.
13. Glaze it with a varnish (or clear nail polish) for protection and a glossy look.
14. Place a kosher mezuzah scroll inside, and hang with 2 nails on your door-post.

Chicken Noodle Soup

Meat

Ingredients:
12 cups of water
2 pounds chicken parts (thighs, breasts, legs)
1 large onion
5 celery stalks
5 large carrots
4 cloves garlic
1 tablespoon dried thyme leaves
1 tablespoon salt
12 ounces egg noodles

Directions:
1. Place chicken in a large soup pot. Wash and cut up the carrots and celery into chunks and add to the pot.
2. Chop the onion. Add the chopped onion, garlic, thyme, salt, and water to the pot.
3. Turn the burner on high and cover the pot until it begins to boil. Turn the heat down to medium-low and simmer for 1 to 2 hours.
4. Add the noodles to the soup. Continue cooking until the noodles are done, after 10 to 12 minutes.

Yields: Approximately 10 servings

Chicken Soup is sometimes called the Jewish Penicillin. Perfect to warm you up on a cold winter day, this recipe is a basic chicken soup recipe that you can add your own special touch to.

Yummy Chocolate Chip Cookies

Pareve/Dairy

Ingredients:
1 cup margarine or butter, softened
2 teaspoons vanilla
2 eggs
1 1/2 cups sugar
2 1/2 cups flour
1 teaspoon baking powder
1 cup chocolate chips

Directions:
1. Preheat oven to 350°.
2. In a large bowl, cream margarine and sugar until fluffy. It will work best with an electric mixer. Add vanilla and eggs and mix well.
3. In a separate bowl, mix flour and baking powder, and slowly add it to the creamed mixture.
4. Mix until all flour is mixed into the dough. Add the chocolate chips and mix gently.
5. Drop teaspoonfuls of dough about 2 inches apart onto a cookie-sheet.
6. Bake for 13 to 15 minutes. The tops should still be soft; the cookies will harden once they're out of the oven.

Yields: 4 dozen cookies

Kislev כסלו

The days are getting shorter, and the nights getting longer...it must almost be Chanukah! With so much darkness, it's perfect timing for a holiday that celebrates light.

When we light the Menorah, it reminds us of our job to 'Light Up the Night"! As Jews, we have to be 'lamplighters' and bring the light of Torah and Mitzvot to the world. Just like we add another candle each night of Chanukah, we have to constantly add in our Torah and mitzvot.

How are you a better person today than you were yesterday? How are you a better Jew?

When we light a candle in a dark room, that tiny flame lights up the whole room. The same is true with any Mitzvah. No matter how small your action seems, it can make a huge difference and light up someone else's whole day.

What can you do to light up someone's day?

Great Dates!

13 - Talmud Bavli completed
14 - Reuven, the oldest tribe, was born
25 - *Chanukah*
      Mishkan completed
26 - First synagogue, Touro Synagogue, dedicated in the USA in 1763

Materials:
3x12" mirror (or two 3x6")
20 flat decorative stones
Hot glue gun
9 3/8-inch hex nuts

In my family we have a collection of all the menorahs we've made throughout the years. We try to light a different one each night! This one is the newest addition...

Directions:
1. Plug in the hot glue gun and wait for it to warm up. Be careful and have an adult help you -- it's very hot.
2. If you're using 2 mirrors for the base, glue them together.
3. Glue 9 stones, evenly spaced, in a straight line, to the mirror.
4. Glue a second stone on top of each of the stones.
5. Glue two more stones to the middle stone. This will be your Shamash.
6. Glue a nut on top of each stack of stones.
7. Let dry, and insert regular-sized Chanukah candles into each nut when you're ready to light it!

Latke Shapes
Pareve

Latkes can be hard and messy to fry, so here's a much simpler, healthier -- and cuter version!

Ingredients:
5 large potatoes, peeled
1 onion
3 eggs
1/3 cup flour
1 teaspoon salt
Pepper to taste
Oil

Directions:
1. Grate potatoes and onion finely with a grater, food processor, or blender.
2. Strain through a colander, pressing out extra water. Add eggs, flour, salt, and pepper, and mix well.
3. Grease a cookie sheet well and place Chanukah-shaped cookie cutters on it. Pour batter into the cookie cutters, making sure to fill each shape. Carefully remove the cookie cutters; the batter should retain its shape. Drizzle with oil and bake at 350° for about half an hour or until golden brown and crispy.

Yields: 4 to 6 servings

Snowball Cookies

Pareve/Dairy

Ingredients:
1/2 cup margarine or butter
2 cups sugar
4 eggs
2 teaspoons baking powder
1 teaspoon vanilla
4 cups flour
4 ounces bittersweet chocolate, melted
Confectioners' sugar

Directions:
1. In a large bowl, cream margarine and sugar. Add eggs and mix well.
2. Mix in baking powder and vanilla.
3. Add flour and melted chocolate well. Mix until completely blended.
4. Refrigerate covered for at least 2 hours.
5. Preheat oven to 375°.
6. Spoon out teaspoon-sized balls, and roll them in confectioners' sugar until completely coated.
7. Place about 3 inches apart on a greased cookie-sheet.
8. Bake for 10 to 12 minutes.

Yields: 5 dozen cookies

Tevet טבת

Although the beginning days of Tevet include the final days of Chanukah, it's a month without holidays. When we were choosing crafts and recipes, we decided on the theme of Shabbat for the month of Tevet. So here are a few thoughts on Shabbat:

All week long we are creators. We write, we cook, we build, we paint. Shabbat is our day to step back and be a creation. To realize that we're not actually as big as we think we are. The world continues running, even without our input. Because Hashem is in charge. Once a week we have that reminder: "I'm not the one in charge. G-d runs the world." That's a very reassuring thought, because Hashem knows how to run the world much better than we do.

When we're rushing through the week, it's easy to take things for granted. Shabbat is also a day to step back and appreciate what we have: A loving family; good health; a comfortable home; delicious food.

How can you show gratitude to Hashem? What are you thankful for?

Great Dates!

1 - Esther made queen
10 - Siege on Yerushalayim - *fast day*
20 - Rambam's passing
    First Talmud Bavli printed

Classic Rugelach

Pareve

Ingredients:

Dough:
- 4 eggs
- 3/4 cup sugar
- 1 cup oil
- 2 teaspoons vanilla
- 6 cups flour
- 4 teaspoons baking powder
- 1 cup orange juice

Filling:
- 4 tablespoons oil
- 1 tablespoon cinnamon and 1 cup sugar (or 1/2 cup cocoa and 1 cup sugar)

Directions:
1. In a large bowl, mix together eggs, sugar, oil, and vanilla.
2. In a separate bowl, combine flour and baking powder. Add a little at a time to the first mixture, alternating between adding the dry mixture and adding orange juice. Mix well.
3. Refrigerate dough for at least one hour.
4. Preheat oven to 325°. On a floured board or very clean counter, roll out the dough to a circle about 1/8 inch thick. Spread a very thin layer of oil over the circle, leaving a 1/2 inch margin around the outside and in the center.
5. Mix cinnamon/cocoa and sugar. Spread over the oil. Cut like a pizza into 12 to 18 triangles.
5. Roll each triangle from the outside edge inward to form the 'rugelach' shape. (Optional: brush each cookie with beaten egg yolk).
6. Place on greased cookie sheet and bake for 15 minutes.

Yields: 6 dozen small rugelach

Ingredients:
- 8 ounces egg noodles
- 3 eggs
- 1/4 cup orange juice
- 1/3 cup sugar
- 1/4 cup applesauce
- 1/2 teaspoon salt
- 4 medium sized apples, sliced
- 4 tablespoons margarine or butter
- 2 teaspoons cinnamon
- 1 tablespoon sugar

This sweet kugel is always a Shabbat favorite. For variety you can substitute peaches, apricots or other fruits instead of apples!

Directions:
1. Preheat oven to 350° and grease an 8-inch pan.
2. Fill a large pot 3/4 of the way with water. Turn on high and cover the pot. When the water is boiling, add the noodles and cook according to the directions on the package.
3. In a large bowl, combine eggs, orange juice, sugar, applesauce, and salt. Mix well.
4. When the noodles are done, turn off the burner, and drain them into a strainer in the sink. Ask an adult to help you - it's very hot!
5. Place the hot noodles back into the pot along with the margarine. Mix. Add the egg mixture and apples to the noodles and mix again.
6. Pour the mixture into the greased pan. In a small bowl, mix the cinnamon and sugar and sprinkle on top of the kugel.
7. Bake for 45 minutes.

Yields: about 8 servings

Shabbat Candlestick

Materials:
2 1.5 inch terra cotta pots
Acrylic paint
Hot glue gun
Other decorations like rhinestones or sequins
Paintbrush
Glue
Tea light

Directions:
1. With an adult's help, use the hot glue gun to glue the pots one on top of the other, with the bottom pot upside-down. Let dry.
2. Paint the pots with whatever colors or designs you like, with acrylic paint and a paintbrush. Let dry.
3. Glue on any other decorations such as rhinestones, ribbon, or sequins. You can really get creative with this step.
4. Put a tea light in the top, and you have your own Shabbat candlestick to light, to welcome the Shabbat on Friday evening.

Lighting Shabbat candles to welcome Shabbat is a special Mitzvah just for Jewish women and girls. Make your own personalized candlestick to light with your mother.

Shvat שבט

Happy Birthday trees! Although it's still winter in the USA, in Israel the trees are already beginning to blossom. Tu B'shvat is the birthday of the trees. But maybe it's your birthday too! Did you know that the Torah compares people to trees? First of all, a tree can't stand tall without strong roots. We have to make sure that our connection to our Jewish roots is strong. We have to learn about our roots-- where we come from--and connect to our great ancestors and heritage.

A tree also gives fruit. Our fruits are the good deeds that we do. The fruits of the tree produce seeds, enabling more trees to grow. Our mitzvot each start a chain-reaction of goodness in the world. After our life is over, these seeds of goodness that we've left behind continue to grow.

Trees, unlike other plants, are constantly growing, even during the harsh winter. Each year, another ring is added onto the tree's trunk. We have to be like trees and constantly be growing and developing into a better person and a better Jew, even during the hard 'seasons' of our life.

What 'ring' did you add to your life this year?

How are you growing this year to be better than you were last year?

Did you know you can plant a tree in Israel, even if you don't live there? Check out www.jnf.org!

Great Dates!

1 - Moshe began repeating the Torah to the Jewish people
15 - *Tu B'Shvat - Birthday of the Trees*
20 - Asher, Yaakov's son was born

Broccoli Trees

Pareve/Dairy

This recipe is a great way to make veggies more exciting for young, picky eaters!

Directions:
1. Thoroughly wash the broccoli and check for bugs.
2. Cut off the hard bottom of the broccoli stalks, and cut the stalks into mini 'trees'.
3. Using a steamer, steam broccoli over boiling water until it is bright green. Rinse, drain, and set aside.
4. Preheat oven to 325°. Lightly grease a 9x14 inch pan.
5. Melt butter (or heat oil) in a large frying pan. Add onion and salt, and sauté on medium heat for about 5 minutes. Add lemon juice.
6. Stir in the rice and herbs into greased pan.
7. Arrange broccoli upright in the pan. Cover loosely with foil and bake for 15 to 20 minutes. Serve hot.

Yields: about 6 servings

Ingredients:
1 bunch broccoli
1 tablespoon butter or oil
1 cup chopped onion
1 teaspoon salt
Juice of 1 lemon
About 6 cups cooked rice
Herbs and spices to taste: black pepper, dill, mint, parsley

Date Nut Bars

Pareve/Dairy

Ingredients:
4 ounces dates, chopped finely
1/2 cup sugar
1/2 cup raisins
1/2 cup walnuts, chopped
1 teaspoon cinnamon
1/4 cup butter or margarine
1 egg
1 cup flour
1 teaspoon baking powder
1 tablespoon orange juice
1 teaspoon vanilla

Directions:
1. Preheat oven to 350°.
2. In a medium bowl, mix dates, sugar, raisins, walnuts, cinnamon. Set aside.
3. In a large bowl cream margarine and eggs. Mix well with flour and baking powder. Add orange juice and vanilla and mix.
4. Fold date mixture into the batter.
5. Form into a loaf shape on a lightly greased cookie sheet.
6. Bake for 15 to 20 minutes. When cool, cut into 1-inch bars.

Yields: 1 loaf

Striped Flower Pot

Materials:
Multiple colors of tissue paper
A terra-cotta flower pot
Liquid glue
Water
Paintbrush

Directions:
1. Cut tissue paper into 1-inch wide strips.
2. In a small bowl, mix water and glue so you have a runny mixture.
3. With the paintbrush, brush a thin layer of glue onto the pot. Place a tissue paper strip on it.
4. Continue until the pot is covered with tissue paper strips. Brush glue mixture over the strips, and continue to add as many layers as you want.
5. Plant some beautiful flowers for Tu B'shvat!

Adar אדר

"The *miracle* of Purim"…"*Hashem* saved the Jewish people"…it's likely that you'll hear these phrases said about Purim. But did you know that Hashem's name isn't mentioned once in the Megillah? In fact, if you read the story of Purim, there aren't any splitting seas or plagues of darkness. It seems like the whole story happened naturally, without Hashem intervening. Just a bunch of coincidences. But if we look carefully, it's obvious how every event was part of Hashem's master plan.

Our lives are like the Megillah. We can see a bunch of coincidences. Or if we look closely, we can discover the hand of G-d. When Hashem splits seas it's easy for everyone to recognize who's in charge. But when we recognize those miracles within everyday life -- that means a lot.

What everyday miracles happen in your life?

Did something ever happen to you where you only realized afterwards why it was meant to happen?

Great Dates!

- 1 - Plague of darkness
- 3 - Second Beit Hamikdash finished
- 7 - Moshe's birth & passing
- 9 - First time Hillel & Shammai had an argument
- 11 - First printing of Rashi's commentary
- 13 - *The fast of Esther*
- 14 - *Purim*
- 15 - *Shushan Purim*
- 17 - Shulchan Aruch - Code of Jewish Law - completed
- 18 - First Jewish periodical published in the US in 1823
- 29 - Jews Commanded first Mitzvah: Rosh Chodesh

Themed Mishloach Manot

Everyone loves Mishloach Manot with a cute theme! Here's a 'Seven Days of Creation' theme. Use our ideas for each day of creation, or your own!

Day 1: Dark/Light - Black & White Cookie
Day 2: Sky & Ocean - Water Bottle
Day 3: Plants & Trees - Orange
Day 4: Sun, Stars & Moon - Star Cookies
Day 5: Birds & Fish - Gummy Fish
Day 6: Animals & People - Animal Crackers
Day 7: Shabbat - Tea Lights

Pack everything inside a blue gift bag, and decorate with green permanent marker to look like the earth.
You can include a note that says something like this:

Have a bite of day and night
Taste a sparkly starry thing
All the wonders of creation
To you this little bag does bring!

We CREATED this special gift to say
Have a very happy Purim day!

Challenge! Can you come up with a YALDAH themed Mishloach Manot?!

Hamentashen

Pareve

Ingredients:
1 cup sugar
4 eggs
1/2 cup oil
1/2 cup lemon juice
1 teaspoon vanilla
5 cups flour
2 teaspoons baking powder
Chocolate chips or jam for filling

Directions:
1. Preheat oven to 350°.
2. Beat sugar and eggs together. Mix in oil, lemon juice, vanilla, flour, and baking powder. Mix well.
3. Using a rolling pin, roll out the dough to about 1/8 inch thick. Using a cookie cutter (or the rim of a cup), cut out 3-inch circles.
4. Spoon 1/2 teaspoon of filling in the middle of each circle. Lift up the right and left sides of the circle and pinch together. Lift the last side up, and pinch all three edges together to form a triangle.
5. Bake on greased cookie sheets for 20 minutes.

Yields: 5 dozen cookies

Gefilte "Fishies"

Pareve

Ingredients:
1 frozen Gefilte fish loaf
Carrots
Frozen peas
A jar of tomato sauce

Directions:
1. Bake the Gefilte fish according to the package's baking instructions. Add a few carrots in the pan.
2. When ready to serve, slice the loaf into 1/2 inch thick slices.
3. On each individual plate, spoon out tomato sauce and spread to use as your background.
4. Lay the piece of Gefilte fish on top of the tomato sauce. Using a sharp knife (with an adult's help) gently cut a triangle from the top and bottom of the slice, forming the fish tail.
5. Press a pea in the place of the eye. Slice the carrot and place the slices in the sauce as bubbles.

Both kids and adults will love this cute variation of a traditional food. Did you know that the fish is the symbol for the month of Adar?

Yields: 8-10 slices

Nissan ניסן

Moving along from Purim, where Esther is the heroine, we come to another holiday where women took the center stage: Pesach. Our sages tell us, "In the merit of the righteous women the Jewish people were freed from Egypt." So what was so righteous about the Jewish women in Egypt? Even while immersed in Egyptian culture, they didn't change their Jewish dress, their names, or language. Throughout Jewish history we have lived in many different cultures, yet we remained a separate nation. It was the strength of the Jewish women that kept us from assimilating in Egypt, and it's that special power that Jewish women have today. The power to stand strong in our Jewish identity, and not be afraid to be different.

How do you make sure to stay strong to your Jewish identity?

At the splitting of the Red Sea, the Jewish women danced with tambourines. Where did slaves in Egypt get tambourines from? While the Jews were enslaved, the Jewish women had faith that there would soon be a miracle to celebrate, and they made tambourines. Even when times looked dark, they trusted Hashem that it would soon be over.

Sometimes when things seem bad, we just have to trust Hashem that it's going to turn out good.

What times in your life have you needed to trust in G-d?

Great Dates!

8 - Achashverosh's 180-day feast ended in Shushan
10 - Miriam's passing
14 - Rambam born
15 - *Pesach*
    Jews left Egypt
21 - Red Sea split
24 - First Shabbat celebrated

Ingredients:
2 large ripe mangos
1/2 honeydew
2 oranges
About 2 tablespoons lemon juice

Directions:
1. Cut the mangos, honeydew, and oranges into bite-sized pieces and mix together in a large bowl.
2. Squeeze lemon juice over the salad.

Yields: around 12 servings

Fantastic Fruit Salad
Pareve

Easy Meringues
Pareve

Ingredients:
- 3 egg whites
- 1 cup sugar

Meringues are a great snack to munch on family Pesach outings.

Directions:
1. Preheat oven to 250°.
2. Beat egg whites (much easier with an electric beater) until they are soft but hold their shape. Gradually add sugar and beat until stiff.
3. You can add in optional treats like chocolate chips, nuts, or flavoring. Spoon onto foil-lined cookie sheet.
4. Bake for one hour.

Yields: 2 dozen meringues

Seder Plate

Materials:
A Pesach design, drawing or photograph
2 sturdy clear plastic plates
Hot glue gun
Liquid glue
Scissors
Paint brush

Directions:
1. Lay your artwork face down and place one of the plates on top of it. Trace around the plate in pencil on the back of the artwork.
2. Cut out the artwork following the guide you just drew.
3. Using the paintbrush, paint the surface of one of the plates with liquid glue.
4. Carefully lay down your cut-out artwork on the plate with glue.
5. With the hot glue gun, make a thin line of glue around the perimeter of the artwork.
6. Plate the other plate on top, lined up with the bottom plate.
7. For the Seder use small glass cups or bowls to place the Seder plate items in, and arrange them on your plate.

Iyar אייר

Have you ever been so excited for something that you counted down the days? Maybe the last day of school? After the Jewish people left Egypt, they counted 49 days until they received the Torah.

They may have been excited, but were they ready to receive this incredible gift from Hashem? Not really. Each day of the 49 days, the Jewish people worked on improving one small part of their character. Maybe it was kindness, maybe humility, or compassion. 49 days later they were a new nation, committed to doing Hashem's will and ready to receive the Torah.

Every year we follow in their footsteps, and count our own 49 days. It's a time to reflect on our personalities. *Are you a very giving person? Self-disciplined? A leader? What are your weaknesses?* A giving person has to learn when to set limits. Someone disciplined has to practice giving without limit. A leader might need to work on humility.

It's hard to change your character. A person can't wake up one morning and decide to be a new person with a new personality. It takes a long time to change. The actions we do shape our character. You want to be more giving? Act like a giving person. You want to be a leader? Talk like a leader would talk.

What are your unique strengths and weaknesses?

What small actions can you take to change yourself for the better?

Great Dates!

- **1** - Construction of second Beit Hamikdash began
- **5** - State of Israel proclaimed
- **14** - *Pesach Sheini*
- **18** - *Lag B'Omer*
  Plague among Rabbi Akiva's students ended
  Passing of Rabbi Shimon Bar Yochai
- **20** - Journey from Har Sinai
- **26** - Israel's Six Day War

Omer Counter

Materials:
Shoe-box lid
7 pipecleaners
49 large beads
Decorative paper
Ruler
Scissors
Glue
Tape
Pencil

Directions:
1. Using your pencil and ruler, make a dot at each corner 1-inch from the edge. Use the ruler to draw a rectangle connecting the dots so you have an even frame.
2. Using scissors or a razor knife (with an adult's help) cut out the inner rectangle you created. You'll be left with a 1-inch wide frame around an empty rectangle.
3. Decorate the frame with decorative paper and stickers.
4. Thread 7 beads onto each pipe cleaner.
5. Turn the frame over and lay the pipe cleaners down vertically, parallel to each other. Tape the beaded pipe cleaners to the inside of the frame.
6. Turn over and hang on a wall. When you start counting the Omer have all the beads on the top of the pipe-cleaner. As you count, move one bead from top to bottom every day. Each time you finish a week, move on to the next pipe-cleaner.

On Lag B'Omer it's customary to have bonfires. Put yourself in the bonfire mood with these yummy s'more cupcakes!

S'more Cupcakes

Pareve/Dairy

Ingredients:
1 cup graham cracker crumbs (about 5 graham crackers, crushed)
1/2 cup flour
1 1/2 teaspoons baking powder
1/2 cup butter or margarine, softened
1 cup sugar
2 eggs plus 1 egg white
2 teaspoons vanilla
8 marshmallows, cut in half
15 squares of chocolate

Directions:
1. Preheat oven to 375°.
2. Mix together graham cracker crumbs, flour, and baking powder.
3. In a medium bowl, mix margarine and sugar together until creamy. Add eggs and vanilla and mix well.
4. Spoon into muffin pans lined with paper baking cups. Fill them about 1/3 full. Place half a marshmallow and a chocolate square on top of each.
5. Bake for 18 to 20 minutes. Cool before serving.

Yields: 15 to 18 regular sized cupcakes

Veggie Kabobs
Pareve

Ingredients:
1 zucchini
2 peppers (different colors)
1 onion
Mushrooms
Oil
Wooden skewers

Directions:
1. Preheat oven to 375°.
2. Slice vegetables into thin slices.
3. Stack vegetable slices onto wooden skewers.
4. Place on a foil-covered cookie-sheet and drizzle with oil.
5. Bake for 15-20 minutes until vegetables are slightly browned.
6. Serve hot.

Yields: 6 kabobs

Sivan סיון

Do you remember Har Sinai? I don't. But apparently my soul does. In fact, your soul does too! Our tradition tells us that all the Jewish souls who were alive at the time, or would be born in the future, were present at the giving of the Torah. But it doesn't always feel like the Torah was given personally to me or you.

Shavuot is that time once a year to receive the Torah anew, and to really make it *yours*. Does your life revolve around the Torah -- our G-d-given instruction manual for life? Is Torah something that excites you? Something that's sweet and enjoyable to learn?

Every morning we recite the blessing "Noten Hatorah" "Blessed are You O Lord, Who *gives* the Torah." We say 'Who *gives* the Torah', in present tense, not 'Who gave the Torah' because G-d is personally giving us the Torah each and every day. It's up to us to make sure that we treat the Torah like a brand-new gift we've received. Are we excited about learning Torah? Do we constantly want to know more? Shavuot is the time to make sure that *every day* we 'receive' the Torah with new enthusiasm.

Do you appreciate what a great gift the Torah is?

How can you make time every day for a little bit of Torah learning?

Great Dates!

- **3** - Jews prepared to receive the Torah
- **5** - Jews accepted the Torah
- **6** - *Shavuot - giving of the Torah*
  Passing of King David
  Passing of the Baal Shem Tov
- **23** - Haman's decree counteracted
- **29** - Spies sent out to Israel

Blintz Loaf

Dairy

Ingredients:

Batter:
1/2 cup butter or margarine, melted
2 eggs
1 teaspoon baking powder
3 tablespoons sugar
1/2 cup milk
1 3/4 cups flour

Filling:
1 pound cottage cheese
2 tablespoons butter or margarine, softened
1 egg
1 tablespoon sour cream, optional
1 teaspoon salt
2 tablespoons sugar
1/2 cup cream cheese

Directions:
1. Preheat oven to 350°. Grease a 9x5-inch loaf pan.
2. Combine the batter ingredients and mix until smooth. Pour 1/2 of the batter into the pan.
3. Mix together all the filling ingredients. Pour over batter and spread gently.
4. Pour the rest of the batter over the filling.
5. Bake for 1 hour.

Yields: about 6 servings

Cheesecake Squares

Dairy

It's customary to have dairy on Shavuot, so of course cheesecake is a favorite. Here's a little variation to the classic cheesecake.

Ingredients:

Crust:
10 graham crackers
1/4 cup sugar
1/2 cup butter or margarine, softened

Filling:
3 eggs
3/4 cup sugar
12 ounces cream cheese
2 teaspoons vanilla

Directions:

Crust:
1. Crush graham crackers until completely ground. You can crush them in a blender or a tightly-sealed bag.
2. Add sugar and margarine and mix well.
3. Press into the bottom of a 9x13-inch pan to create the crust. Refrigerate.

Filing:
1. Preheat oven to 375°.
2. Beat eggs in a small bowl. Add sugar, cream cheese, and vanilla and mix well. Pour into crust.
3. Bake for 20 minutes. Turn off the oven and leave the bars in for one hour. Remove and cool.

Yields: 24 medium-sized squares

Mosaic Placemat

Materials:
Old magazines and photos of flowers and nature
Scissors
Glue
A large (placemat sized) piece of paper

Directions:
1. Go through old magazines and photos and cut out any pictures with flowers, leaves, or greenery in them.
2. Cut all the photos into small shapes and shards.
3. Sort the pieces into piles according to color.
4. On the large white paper, outline a design you'd like. It could be a flower like we did, an abstract design, or a scene like Mount Sinai.
5. Brush glue over the whole white paper.
6. Fill in the design by placing the picture pieces on the glue.
7. Let dry. To make it sturdier, take your placemat to a copy store and have it laminated.

On Shavuot we decorate synagogues and homes with flowers, to remind us how Har Sinai blossomed with flowers when the Torah was given. Give a flowery touch to you table with this mosaic placemat.

Tammuz תמוז

Have you ever read a book where you actually felt as if you were in the castle, or the spaceship, or the island that was being described? You could almost reach out and touch it...

In Tammuz we're faced with a challenge. We're supposed to mourn for three weeks, culminating on Tisha B'av, for the destruction of the Beit Hamikdash, two thousand years ago. For me it's pretty hard to mourn something I never saw, and can't really imagine. Ok, I know the Beit Hamikdash was a very special place, a very holy place. But really, what's that got to do with my life?

That's why during this mourning period there is a custom to learn all about the Beit Hamikdash -- all its laws, how it looked, its dimensions. The Beit Hamikdash isn't just about mourning the past. It's about envisioning the future. Soon, with the final Redemption, we'll be able to rebuild the Beit Hamikdash in Jerusalem, and once again we'll have a place in the world shining with holiness, truth, and clarity. A place where the Divine can dwell. And the more I learn about it, the more real it becomes. I can almost reach out and touch it...

What do you know about the Beit Hamikdash? How can you learn more?

What part of the Beit Hamikdash is most special to you?

Great Dates!

3 - Yehoshua stopped the sun
9 - Jerusalem walls breached
16 - Golden calf made
17 - *Fast of 17 Tammuz*
18 - Golden calf destroyed
29 - Passing of Rashi

Memory Frame

Materials:
Shoebox
Photograph
Construction paper or patterned scrapbook paper
Glue
Scissors
Photos, memorabilia, ticket stubs, and anything special you want to remember

Directions:
1. Cover the shoebox with construction paper or scrapbook paper and glue down.
2. Glue your photo to the center of the box.
3. Cut out words from your memorabilia, special phrases to remember, stickers, and more to decorate the border of your frame.

Summer is a time for memories. Whether it's camp or a family trip, this is a great way record special memories.

Jam Diagonals
Pareve/Dairy

Ingredients:
3/4 cup butter or margarine, softened
3/4 cup brown sugar
1 teaspoon vanilla
1 1/4 cups flour
1/4 teaspoon salt
1 tablespoon baking powder
1 3/4 cups oatmeal
1 1/2 cups jam

Directions:
1. Preheat oven to 350°.
2. Grease and set aside a 9x13-inch pan.
3. In a large bowl, cream butter and sugar. Add vanilla, flour, salt, baking powder and oatmeal. Mix well.
4. Roll the dough into 9-inch ropes. Slightly flatten the ropes until they are around 3 inches wide. Spread jam down the middle of each rope.
5. Bake for 30 minutes on a foil-covered cookie sheet.
6. Let cool. Cut each rope on a diagonal, and continue cutting parallel lines to create diagonal cookies.

Yields: 2 dozen bars

Chicken Salad

Meat

Directions:
Combine all ingredients and chill thoroughly.

Ingredients:
3 cups cooked diced chicken
1 1/2 cup diced apples
1/3 cup chopped celery
1/4 cup raisins
1 tablespoon lemon juice
2/3 cup mayonnaise
1 teaspoon salt

אב Av

Looking back in our Jewish history, the month of Av seems to have more than its share of tragedies. The first day of Av begins the 'The Nine Days' -- a period of mourning preceding the fast day of Tisha B'av. Throughout Jewish history Tisha B'av has been a day of expulsion, persecution, and disaster. We fast every year to remember all these tragedies, and of course the biggest tragedy of all, the destruction of the first and second Beit Hamikdash on Tisha B'av.

So where is the positivity in Av? It's actually on the day of Tisha B'av itself. Even though it's a day of mourning, Tisha B'av is also a day of hope. It's taught that Moshiach, our future redeemer, was born on Tisha B'av. That means that right after the Beit Hamikdash was destroyed, we had the possibility of being redeemed. Close to two thousand years later, we're still waiting. But we haven't lost hope.

We know that every day that goes by means that we're one day closer to the final Redemption, a time when there will be peace on Earth and everyone will recognize Hashem as G-d. We're the ones who are going to make it happen! By keeping strong faith in Moshiach, that makes Moshiach come faster. Every Mitzvah we do brings Moshiach closer.

What mitzvah can you do to bring Moshiach?

Great Dates!

- **1** - Passing of Aharon
- **7** - 1st Beit Hamikdash invaded
- **8** - Spies returned
- **9** - Fall of Betar
   Spanish Expulsion in 1492
   Both Beit Hamikdashs destroyed
   Tisha B'Av Fast Day
- **20** - Zohar published

Sunshine Salad

Pareve

Ingredients:
- 1 can corn, drained
- 1 tomato, diced
- 1 small cucumber, peeled and diced
- 1 green pepper, diced
- 3 tablespoons mayonnaise
- Salt and pepper to taste

Directions:
1. Mix all ingredients.
2. Refrigerate until serving.

Yields: 4 to 6 servings

Strawberry Splash

Dairy

Ingredients:
1 cup frozen strawberries
8 ounces of vanilla or strawberry yogurt
1 1/2 cups of milk

Directions:
Place all ingredients in blender and blend until smooth.

Yields 4 servings

This healthy smoothie is great to cool you down on a hot day!

Rainbow Tote

Materials:
Lightweight tote bag
Colorful fabric scraps
Needle
Thread

Directions:
1. Cut your scraps so they are even squares or rectangles.
2. Lay them down on the front of the bag and decide where you want each piece to go.
3. Thread the needle and tie a knot at the end of the thread. Starting from the back side (inside the bag) pierce the fabric. Continue stitching a simple in-out-in-out stitch (the running stitch) around the edge of the square.
3. When you get to the end of the square, end with the needle inside the bag, and tie a strong knot.
4. Repeat for each square.
5. For a finishing touch, decorate with fabric paint and let dry.

A tote bag is just what you need in the summer for toting to and from camp or the pool. Fill with swim supplies and a good book!

Elul אלול

Wow, this year has really flown by. Can you believe we're already approaching Rosh Hashanah? Throughout the year it's so easy to get busy with schoolwork, friends, camp...and not have a minute to look back. Elul is that month where we slow down and reflect. Without taking the time once in a while to refocus, it's easy to lose focus in life.

What did you accomplish in the past year?
What do you wish you had done differently?
What is one area you want to improve in for the coming year?
What do you hope to accomplish next year?

Luckily for us, it's the easiest time of year to make new resolutions and become closer to Hashem. The entire year, G-d is a King sitting in His palace. Yes, we can have an audience, but it requires traveling far to get to the palace and going through many guards. In Elul the King comes and stands in the field, ready to greet anyone who wants to speak to Him.

G-d is standing right here, waiting for us to come close and ask for what we need. All we have to do is take advantage of the opportunity. Do an extra mitzvah. Put a coin in the tzedakah box. Pick up a siddur and daven from your heart. Ask G-d your questions. Tell Him how you're feeling. Ask for what you need. He's waiting for you.

Great Dates!

2 - Shulchan Aruch - Code of Jewish Law - published
10 - Noach sent out Raven
17 - Noach sent out Dove
25 - 7 days of creation began

Pasta Salad

Pareve

Ingredients:
8 ounces pasta, cooked, rinsed and drained
1 cup mayonnaise
1 cup quartered cherry tomatoes
1 cup chopped, seeded cucumber
2 tablespoons cider vinegar
1 teaspoon dried dill
1 teaspoon salt
1/8 teaspoon pepper

Directions:
1. In a large bowl combine mayonnaise, vinegar, dill, salt and pepper.
2. Add pasta, tomatoes, and cucumbers. Mix well.
3. Cover and chill to serve.

Fabric Pushka

Materials:
An empty can or jar
Cardboard or cardstock
Pencil
Scissors
A patterned knee-sock
Ribbon
Fabric paint

Directions:
1. Stand the jar upside-down on the cardboard and trace around the rim of the jar.
2. Cut out the circle. Cut a slot for coins in the middle of it (ask an adult to help you use a box-cutter), and glue the cardboard to the rim of the jar.
3. Cut small holes in the elastic top of the sock every inch. Weave the ribbon in and out through the holes.
4. Slip the sock over the jar so the top of the sock lines up with the top of the jar. Cut the sock at the bottom of the jar. Tie the ribbon in a bow.
5. Write the Hebrew word Tzedakah or Charity on the front with fabric paint. Let dry.

Marble Cake
Pareve/Dairy

Ingredients:

Cake:
1 cup butter or margarine, softened
2 1/2 cups sugar
4 eggs
3 1/2 cups flour
1/2 teaspoon salt
4 teaspoons baking powder
1 1/3 cups milk or orange juice
2 teaspoons vanilla

Marble:
4 tablespoons cocoa
3 tablespoons sugar
5 tablespoons hot water

Directions:
1. Preheat the oven to 350°.
2. Grease a 9x13-inch cake pan, and set it aside.
3. In a large bowl, cream margarine. Add sugar gradually, then add the eggs.
4. In a separate bowl, mix together the flour, salt, and baking powder. Add to the margarine mixture, alternating between a little of the dry mixture, and a little of the milk/orange juice. Add vanilla and mix.
5. To make the marble, in a small bowl, mix together sugar, cocoa, and hot water.
6. Pour cake batter into greased pan. Drizzle the marble mixture over the batter and run a knife through it with a swirling motion.
7. Bake for 45 to 55 minutes or until a toothpick comes out clean.

Yields: 1 cake

Glossary

Achashveirosh - the Persian king in the times of the Purim story
Adam & Chava - Adam & Eve
Akieidat Yitzchak - the binding of Isaac
Beit Hamikdash - Holy Temple
Har Sinai - Mount Sinai
Hashem - G-d
Hillel & Shammai - two great sages with differing opinions
Imeinu - our mother
Kosher - fit for use according to Jewish law
Menorah - the candelabra used for the holiday of Chanukah
Mezuzah - a scroll affixed to doorposts of Jewish homes
Mitzvah/Mitzvos - commandment, good deed
Moshe - Moses
Moshiach - the anointed one, the person who will usher in the future Redemption
Noach - Noah
Omer - 49 days between Pesach and Shavuot
Pareve - neither dairy or meat
Pesach - Passover
Purim - A holiday celebrating the defeat of Haman's plot to massacre the Jews
Pushka - charity box
Rambam - Maimonides
Rosh Chodesh - the new month
Rosh Hashanah - the new year
Seder - ritual meal on the first two nights of Passover
Shabbat - the Sabbath - from sundown Friday to sunset Saturday
Shamash - the candle on the Menorah that lights the other candles
Shavuot - a holiday celebrating receiving the Torah
Shulchan Aruch - the code of Jewish law
Simchat Torah - a holiday celebrating completing the yearly cycle of reading the Torah
Sukkah - a temporary shelter in honor of the holiday of Sukkot
Sukkot - a holiday celebrating the harvest where we dwell in temporary booths
Tisha B'Av - a fast day mourning the destruction of the Holy Temple
Torah - the Bible
Tu B'shvat - a holiday celebrating the new year of the trees
Yaakov Avinu - Jacob, our forefather
Yehoshua - Joshua
Yerushalayim - Jerusalem
Yom Kippur - a fast day of atonement, the holiest day of the year

Thank you to...

The Larson and Resnick families for allowing us to use your homes and kitchens for The YALDAH Year.

Rochel Larson for always lending a hand and creative eye.

Daniella and Rebecca Wirtschafter, and Rebecca Gopen for your patience and cooperation at the photo shoot.

Friends who were always there to share their favorite recipes, ideas, and tips.

The YALDAH magazine readers who make an incredible community of Jewish girls!

-Leah & Chavie

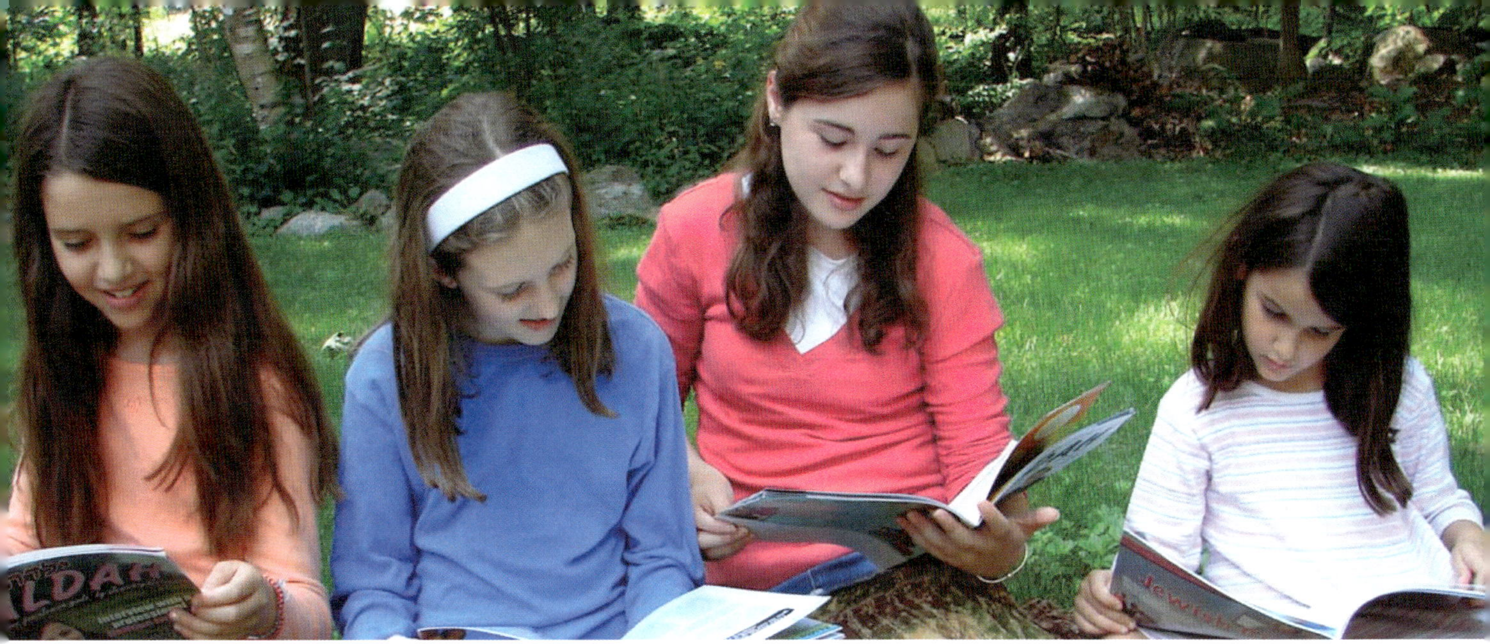

YM Books is a division of YALDAH Media, Inc. YALDAH Media, Inc. is dedicated to providing high-quality, kosher media to Jewish girls of all ages. We celebrate Jewish girls and women, Jewish life and values, and creativity. We aim to connect Jewish girls and inspire them to embrace their Judaism with pride and become Jewish leaders of the future. YALDAH Media, Inc. encourages girls to tap into their hidden talents and pursue their dreams. Through our YM Books, YALDAH magazine, and Jewish Girls Retreats, we inspire girls to change the world.

Visit our website, www.yaldahmedia.com for updates on new books and programs for Jewish girls!

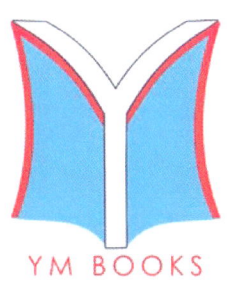

Want more like this book?

More books from YM Books:

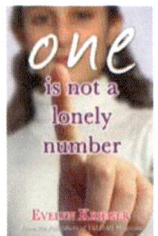

One Is Not A Lonely Number by Evelyn Krieger
Thirteen-year-old Talia Shumacher is the only child of a wealthy orthodox couple, known for their hospitality. As Talia becomes a teenager, her parents' open-door policy begins to irritate her. When Gabrielle Markus, an eccentric twenty-three-year old ballet dancer shows up one day, Talia's life is turned upside down. Convinced that Gabrielle is harboring a secret, Talia and her friends set out to uncover it. Along the way, Talia must deal with the loneliness she feels as an only child living in a religious community that celebrates large families. In discovering Gabrielle's secret, Talia discovers secrets about herself and her parents. Talia's gift for math and her unusual way of thinking about numbers is woven into the story along with themes of friendship, individuality, and acceptance.
Ages 10-15 ~ Paperback

Teen Talk *15 Questions We - Jewish Girls - Wanted Answered* by Chaya Freeman & friends
As teens, we know that teenage life is full of questions. What's my purpose in life? Will I ever get along with my parents? What's wrong with boyfriends? Do I really want this lifestyle I didn't choose? What's so important about school? Should I start planning my future? What do others think of me? How can I help my friend?... So we asked. We asked our friends, wise adults, parents, teachers, other teens -- and ourselves. The result: an honest collage of personal stories, interviews, reflections, questions, and advice to help us navigate the confusion of life as a frum* teenage girl.
Ages 13-18 ~ Paperback
*Although the questions and issues addressed in the book were written with observant Jewish girls in mind, we're sure that the advice, wisdom, and personal stories will touch girls from all Jewish backgrounds.

Qty	Item	Price	Total
	One Is Not A Lonely Number	$12.99	
	Teen Talk	$11.99	
	Shipping	$2.95 (US only)	$2.95
		TOTAL:	$

SHIP TO:
Name:_____
Address:_____
City:_____ State:_____ Zip:_____
Email/phone:_____

Mail this form with a check payable to YALDAH Media, Inc. to YM Books, P.O. Box 215, Sharon, MA 02067.

YALDAH MAGAZINE

YALDAH is a full color, quarterly magazine 'for Jewish girls, by Jewish girls'. Each 64-page issue is full of inspirational, informative, and entertaining reading for Jewish girls including true stories, fiction, interviews, crafts, quizzes, advice, and more. Founded by Leah Larson at age 13, YALDAH shows girls that using their talents and determination, they can make their dreams come true!

☐ **YES!** I want a subscription to YALDAH magazine, the *only* magazine for Jewish girls, *by* Jewish girls! And it's just **$26** for a year (4 issues) or **$45** for 2 years (8 issues)!
Name:_____
Address:_____
City:_____ State:_____ Zip:_____
Email/phone:_____
__ Add me to the YALDAH e-mail list

Mail this form with a check payable to YALDAH Media, Inc. to YM Books, P.O. Box 215, Sharon, MA 02067.
You can also subscribe online at www.yaldahmagazine.com!

Behind the Scenes!

All the crafts and recipes in this book were written, tested, and photographed by girls like you! Here's a peek behind the scenes...

The chief testers: Chavie Resnick & Leah Larson

Our cover photo was actually taken on the kitchen floor!

Leah photographing the sweet-potato pie

Putting the last touches on the Omer Counter

Sneaking a cookie!

Some of the goodies...after a few nibbles!

69

Visit us online at
www.theyaldahyear.com

Crafts, Recipes, and the Jewish Year...

This colorful and fun book gives Jewish girls something creative to do in every month of the year.

Each Jewish month features two recipes and a craft connected to that month, plus lots of interesting background information about the month. Ranging from traditional chicken soup to baked latke shapes, a new twist on an old favorite, to creative Purim basket ideas, how to make a Mezuzah cover, and everything in between.

All craft and recipe directions are simply written with young girls in mind, accompanied by beautiful full-color photographs.

All Ages - Paperback

Made in the USA